WRITING HOME

The Story of
THOMAS WOLFE

LAURA BOFFA

TAYLOR TRADE PUBLISHING
Lanham | Boulder | New York | Toronto | London, UK

Published by Taylor Trade Publishing

An imprint of The Rowman & Littlefield Publishing Group, Inc.

4501 Forbes Boulevard, Suite 200, Lanham, Maryland 20706

Unit A, Whitacre Mews, 26-34 Stannary Street, London SE11 4AB

www.rowman.com

Distributed by NATIONAL BOOK NETWORK

British Library Cataloguing in Publication Information Available

Library of Congress Cataloging-in-Publication Data Available

ISBN 978-1-63076-133-2 (cloth)
ISBN 978-1-63076-134-9 (e-book)

 ™ The paper used in this publication meets the minimum requirements of American National Standard for Information Sciences—Permanence of Paper for Printed Library Materials, ANSI/NISO Z39.48-1992.

THOMAS CLAYTON WOLFE
OCTOBER 3, 1900 - SEPTEMBER 15, 1938

Thomas Wolfe's writing resulted in three more novels and many shorter works, but his first novel, *Look Homeward, Angel*, remains his most famous to this day. In the book, he called the town "Altamont" rather than Asheville, and the Old Kentucky Home mentioned in this book became "Dixieland," but there was no mistaking that the story of a boy named "Eugene Gant" was the tale of Thomas Wolfe's own childhood.

Nearly the whole town turned against Tom when they saw what he'd written about them in his thinly disguised "fiction." Tom felt so unwelcome in Asheville that he later used the book title *You Can't Go Home Again*. But when he did return eight years after the town's angry reception of *Look Homeward, Angel*, Tom found that he had not only been largely forgiven but that the town now embraced him as a local celebrity. When Thomas Wolfe died of tuberculosis of the brain before his 38th birthday, the Old Kentucky Home overflowed with the people of Asheville who now considered Tom to be Asheville's "favorite native son."

"If one wants to write a book that has any interest or any value whatever, he has got to write it out of experience of life. A writer, like everybody else, must use what he has to use."

—*Thomas Wolfe*, You Can't Go Home Again

In loving memory of Auntie Kay,

who was Thomas Wolfe's biggest fan

(and who would argue to the ends of the earth

if you told her otherwise).

A special thanks to Historic Site Manager Tom Muir

and all of the Thomas Wolfe Memorial staff.

Tom threw his Christmas list onto the fire. Orange flames ate the cursive letters. The smoke, his father told him, would carry his Christmas wishes to the North Pole. "Horn" and "slate" and "soldier suit" disappeared up the chimney, showing Tom the magic of writing: that by putting words on a page, his dreams could travel the world.

When Tom grew up, he wrote books that carried millions of words across the world. But books helped Tom come into the world, too. Thomas Wolfe was born from books.

In the late 1800s, a determined woman named Julia Westall sold books around the mountain town of Asheville, North Carolina. People had told her that the stonecutter in town liked to read, so she walked into his monument shop looking for a customer.

Instead she found the man she would marry, William
Oliver, or W.O., Wolfe.

Julia moved into the house that the stonecutter had built with marble steps, a wide wrap-around front porch, and fruit trees in the yard. They had eight children together, and on October 3, 1900, the youngest, Thomas, was born.

W.O. loved to scoop Tom up in his rough hands and toss him into the air or nuzzle him with his scratchy beard.

At dinner, he would poke at Tom's stomach and say, "Ah! There's an empty place." Then he would heap more food onto Tom's plate to fill up the emptiness.

In the wintertime, Tom nestled among his brothers and sisters to listen to their father's theatrical voice as he read Shakespeare. In the warm glow of the fireplace, these stories sparked Tom's love of literature.

Sometimes, the house became heated with W.O.'s angry outbursts. Julia decided to take the youngest Wolfe children away from the stonecutter's hot temper, while the oldest stayed to look after him. When Tom was three, his mother loaded him, his sister Mabel, and his brothers Fred, Grover, and Ben, onto a train. The steam engine carried them past the mountains to the city of St. Louis, home of the World's Fair.

Tom's mother opened a boarding house for fair visitors. Life in the enormous house was exciting for Tom. Every day, he met new people from faraway places.

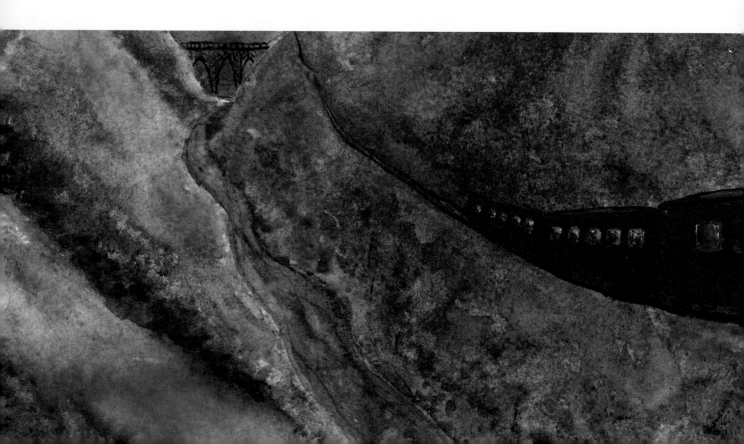

Fred, Ben, Grover, and Mabel took Tom to the fairgrounds each week. He marveled at a life-sized elephant sculpture made of almonds, drank hot tea served by waiters in turbans, and rode a boat through a haunted tunnel.

His favorite was the revolving steam engine in the Palace of Transportation. It gleamed like the train that had brought him to St. Louis.

Grover sold newspapers at the fair. Sickness traveled fast through the crowds, and Grover caught typhoid fever. When the fever took his life, Julia loaded her other children back onto a train to reunite what was left of the Wolfe family. Tom was too young to understand that home would never be the same. He remembered Grover's brown eyes and soft voice in his dreams.

Tom was good at remembering. He could still remember when he was a baby, sitting in a basket on the porch and watching his sister walk up the hill to school. Now, Tom was five years old, and he wanted to go to school too.

He tagged along with his sister and, even though the rules said he was too young to start school, the teacher let him stay and learn.

In the building filled with long halls and so many doors, Tom felt small and lost. His brother Ben helped him learn his way around the school and guarded him against bullies.

Shortly after he started school, Tom's family split apart again. His father worked hard cutting elegant headstones, but his mother claimed that people did not die fast enough to earn a living that way. She missed running her own business, so she bought another boarding house.

Julia bought an eighteen-room house just two blocks from the family home. She kept its original name, The Old Kentucky Home, even though it was in North Carolina. Tom's mother cleaned, cooked meals on a cast-iron stove, and ironed linens from dawn until the late hours of night. It wasn't long before she moved into the boarding house, and she brought Tom with her.

Just like in St. Louis, Tom met new people every day. Asheville's green mountains and fresh air brought travelers from all over, and up to thirty visitors at a time filled the rocking chairs on the front porch or listened to Tom's sister play the piano in the sun room. One guest fixed up the phonograph and taught Tom how to dance.

One morning, Tom woke up and looked out the window. A man was juggling outside. His mother had rented out rooms to an entire circus.

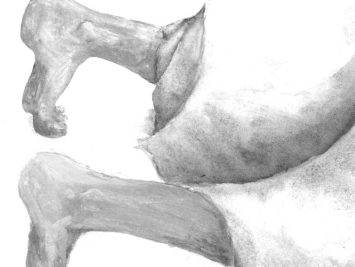

But Tom was older now and no longer thought that living in a boarding house was exciting. He called the big, yellow house ugly and compared the rooms to prison cells. He missed sitting around the fire with his family. Even though Tom was growing fast, his mother did not heap food onto his plate like his father had. She did not fill his empty places.

Instead, Tom's mother put him to work. He passed out business cards, went to the market, and shoveled coal for the Old Kentucky Home. When the ice delivery did not arrive, Tom had to walk to the factory and carry home a twenty-five pound block of ice for his mother's icebox.

Tom did not even have a bedroom. Julia tried to squeeze in as many guests as possible, sometimes putting two strangers in a bed together or setting a mattress out on the porch, and Tom was shuffled around to make room for them. When the boarding house was filled with summer tourists, he was sent back to his father's house. Tom lived under two roofs, but neither house felt like a home.

When his mother was too busy working to take care of Tom, his brother, Ben, picked him up and took him to the diner to eat or made sure he had shoes that fit his quickly growing feet.

Tom outgrew the other boys his age. He was clumsy and uncomfortable in his lanky body. His mother kept his hair in long curls, the style for much younger boys, and Tom had to catch lice on purpose so that she would give him a haircut. Tom struggled with sports, and he spoke with a stammer. Even though he loved to study, Tom did not think he fit in at school.

After school, Tom was in no hurry to return to the boarding house. Instead, he rushed to his father's house, where he would join Ben and Fred around the organ in their playhouse or tell Mabel about school while she fixed him a snack.

Some days, Tom went to the library after school.
Long shelves of leather-scented books reached up toward
the tall ceiling. Tom read quietly in the tower-like turret.
The librarian claimed that Tom read more books than any
other boy in North Carolina. Books carried Tom away from
stammering at school and the strangers and noise of the Old
Kentucky Home. For Tom, books were like trains.

Sometimes, Tom and his mother did ride trains to
faraway places. He loved the beaches of Florida, the spicy
city of New Orleans, and watching President Wilson's
inauguration in Washington, DC. Tom knew that one day he
would live on the other side of Asheville's mountains.
He wondered if writing would take him there.

When Tom was eleven, he entered a writing contest. The principal's wife, Mrs. Roberts, read Tom's essay and cried out that the boy was a genius. The next year, she became his teacher at a new private school, where she introduced Tom to all her favorite books and helped him to develop his own writing style.

Tom dreamed of using his talent to write plays. He tried to become a performer like his father, but it did not come naturally. When he played Prince Hal in the school's Shakespeare pageant, the tights for his costume were too short, so his sister sewed scraps from a clown costume to the bottom. When Prince Hal walked on stage, the audience roared with laughter.

Tom was slow to recover from the humiliation, but he joined the debate team and stood in front of an audience again. Although he stammered through his performances, his team won every debate. When Tom recited an essay he had written about Shakespeare's life, he won first prize. Despite his struggle speaking, it was becoming clear that Tom had a way with words.

W.O. had high hopes for Tom, so he sent him on a train across the state to the University of North Carolina. Most people, including Tom's family, did not believe that working class, small town boys could become writers, and his father insisted that he study law instead, but Tom was determined. He spent his time editing the college newspaper, publishing poems in the university magazine, and writing and performing in plays.

Tom returned to the mountains when his mother wrote him that Ben was sick. Helpless, he watched his brother, who had protected him at school and taken care of him at home, die from pneumonia in the Old Kentucky Home. Tom claimed that the Asheville he knew died with his brother.

Books had been like the train that took Tom away from Asheville when he was young. Now, writing was like the train that brought him home. After college, Tom went on to Harvard University, lived in Boston and New York, and traveled through Europe, but he spent all of his time there writing thousands of pages about the home he had before Ben died, before he moved into his mother's boarding house apart from his family, and even before he lost his brother Grover in St. Louis.

Tom filled his first book, *Look Homeward, Angel,*
with warm moments gathered around the fireplace and
the encouraging voice of his teacher. He also wrote about
the dirty yellow boarding house that surrounded him
with strangers instead of family, the house where he had
watched his brother die.

Tom wrote about more than 200 people from his life,
and not everything he wrote was kind. He wrote about the
ugly side of life as well as the beautiful side, recreating home
just as he remembered it.

Tom called his book fiction and changed the characters'
names, but the people of Asheville recognized themselves
and were outraged. Tom received violent threats. His own
book was banned from the library where he had once tried
to read every book on the shelves.

Tom felt he could not go home, so he kept home with
him by writing thousands of pages about it. Across the world,
Tom's books showed readers his mountain town home and
introduced them to its people. The small town writer was
becoming a big success.

When Tom finally decided to return to Asheville, he was surprised to find that nearly everyone had forgiven him for his first book. This time, when Thomas Wolfe looked homeward, he was welcomed as a hero. Like a train, his books had carried him there.